Contents

Front cover View of the Museum showing the 15-inch guns from HMS *Resolution* (left) and HMS *Ramillies* (right)
Back cover The exterior of the Bethlem Royal Hospital at Lambeth Road, London, pre-1914
Left View of the atrium

Welcome to the Imperial War Museum

The Imperial War Museum was founded in 1917 in order to ensure future generations understood the causes, and most importantly the consequences, of the First World War. Its remit has been extended over the years to cover subsequent conflicts.

Today it is a major national museum, chronicling the impact of war at all levels – from the home front in Britain to the front line, wherever British and Commonwealth forces have seen action in the twentieth and twenty-first centuries.

The Museum is home to unparalleled collections supporting the themes we cover – from ration books to Viscount Montgomery's caravans at our Duxford branch. The Imperial War Museum is also a major art gallery, national archive and a centre for research.

Our five branches currently host some two million visitors a year, with a further ten million getting to know us through our website. We are committed to increasing access to a wider range of audiences with diverse needs through an extensive programme of award-winning exhibitions and educational programmes.

At Imperial War Museum London, there are six floors of exhibitions and displays to explore. My particular recommendations include *The Holocaust Exhibition* and the *Trench* and *Blitz Experiences*, but there is undoubtedly something for everyone. We also have a lively daily programme of activities and events.

For the future, we are not only planning to expand our offer by redisplaying key galleries with more of the personal stories of those involved in conflict, but also to make our research facilities more accessible, particularly for those new to the subject. We hope this will give you many reasons to come back to the Museum again and again.

The Museum also has two other branches in London, HMS *Belfast* and Churchill Museum and Cabinet War Rooms. HMS *Belfast* is moored on the River Thames, next to Tower Bridge, and is the largest object in our Collections. The *Belfast* supported the advancing Allied troops on D-Day, 6 June 1944, and has nine decks of living history to explore.

Churchill Museum and Cabinet War Rooms is housed in the underground complex where Winston Churchill and his Cabinet met in 1940 as the bombs rained down on London. This innovative museum is the world's first major museum dedicated to the life of Winston Churchill.

Outside London, the Museum is fortunate to have Imperial War Museum Duxford, near Cambridge, considered to be Europe's premier aviation museum. Our fifth branch is Imperial War Museum North in Manchester, which is housed in a powerful building designed by Daniel Libeskind, representative of the world torn apart by conflict.

Finally, I would like to emphasise that the Museum relies greatly on support of all kinds: from the Friends of the Imperial War Museum and our amazing teams of volunteers, through to those people who support us with donations and legacies. If you would like to help us, please visit our website for further details, **www.iwm.org.uk**.

Thank you, and please visit us again soon.

Diane Lees

Diane Lees, Director-General

History of the Museum and Bethlem Royal Hospital

In 1917 the Cabinet decided that a National War Museum should be set up to collect and display material relating to the Great War, which was then still being fought. The interest taken by the Dominion governments led to the museum being given the title of Imperial War Museum. It was formally established by Act of Parliament in 1920 and a governing Board of Trustees appointed.

The Museum was opened in the Crystal Palace by King George V on 9 June 1920. From 1924 to 1935 it was housed, under very difficult conditions, in two galleries adjoining the former Imperial Institute, South Kensington.

On 7 July 1936, the Duke of York, shortly to become King George VI, reopened the Museum in its present home. The Museum was closed to the public from September 1940 to November 1946 and vulnerable collections were evacuated to stores outside London. Most of the exhibits survived the war, but a Short seaplane, which had flown at the Battle of Jutland, was shattered when a German bomb fell on the Naval Gallery on 31 January 1941, and some of the naval models were damaged by the blast.

At the outset of the Second World War, the Museum's terms of reference were expanded to cover both world wars, and they were again extended in 1953 to include all military operations in which Britain or the Commonwealth have been involved since August 1914.

The building which accommodates the Museum was formerly the central portion of Bethlem Royal Hospital, or 'Bedlam'. Designed by James Lewis, it was completed in 1815. Sidney Smirke's dome was added in 1846 and contained the chapel. The east and west wings were demolished in the early 1930s to make room for the park which now surrounds the Museum.

Bethlem Royal Hospital dates back to 1247, when Simon Fitz-Mary, a wealthy alderman and a sheriff of London, founded the Priory of St Mary of Bethlehem on the site which is now part of Liverpool Street station. In the fourteenth century, the priory began to specialise in the care of the insane. In 1547 Henry VIII granted the hospital to the City of London.

Bethlem was moved to a new building in Moorfields in 1676. Until 1770 there were no restrictions on visitors, and the patients, who were often manacled or chained to the walls, were a public attraction.

The hospital was housed in the present building from 1815 to 1930, when it was transferred to Eden Park near Beckenham, Kent.

Patients included Mary Nicholson, who tried to assassinate George III in 1786; Jonathan Martin, committed in 1829 after setting fire to York Minster; the painters Richard Dadd and Louis Wain, the latter famous for his cartoons of cats; Antonia White, author of *Frost in May* and *Beyond the Glass*; and the architect AWN Pugin, who designed the Houses of Parliament and St George's Roman Catholic Cathedral opposite the Museum.

Above Imperial War Museum London, 2008 **Left** Corridor of Bethlem Royal Hospital © Photograph reproduced by permission of the Bethlem Art and History Collections Trust, IWM BED 10

Below left Poster designed by Edward Wadsworth for the Imperial War Museum, Lambeth, c.1936 © Transport for London, IWM PST 4624 **Below right** Bethlem Hospital as it was in 1843 IWM MH 3478

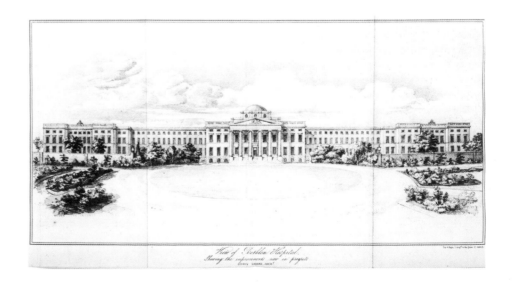

Military Weapons

Above 18-pounder field gun
Left View of the Large Exhibits Gallery

Above 'J' Battery, Royal Horse Artillery, in open positions, 1914 IWM Q 60751

The Large Exhibits Gallery, the impressive central space of the redevelopment of the original building, is the setting for some of the most important weapons and vehicles in the Collections, including guns, tanks and aircraft. Examples of several of the artillery pieces used in the world wars can be seen. The 18-pounder was the standard British field gun and earned a reputation as one of the most reliable weapons of its type. Nearly 100 million rounds of 18-pounder ammunition were expended in France alone between 1914 and 1918, an average of 43 rounds for every minute of the war. The 75mm, the French equivalent of the 18-pounder, was the first gun to be fitted with a recoil system and was renowned for its accuracy and rapidity of fire.

Heavy artillery includes a British 9.2-inch howitzer and a 60-pounder gun, which had a range of seven miles.

An unusual observation device is a German mast periscope designed for use behind buildings and in woods.

The tank – a British invention – was developed to break the deadlock of trench warfare. The Mark V represented an important advance in tank design. Introduced in 1918, it carried a crew of eight and could travel at a speed of over 4 miles per hour.

The earliest of the five Second World War tanks in the gallery is the British Infantry Mark II 'Matilda', a type which gave a good account of itself in France in 1940 and against the Italians in the Western Desert in the winter of 1940–1941. The German 8.8cm was the only anti-tank gun able to penetrate its thick armour plating. The arrival of the M3 Grant in the Western Desert in the summer of 1942 at last gave the hard-pressed British Eighth Army a tank which could match the Panzer Mark IIIs and IVs of the German Afrika Korps. The slow but heavily armoured Churchill was one of the more successful British tanks and saw service in Tunisia, Italy and North-West Europe. The principal armoured weapon of the Allied armies was the American-built M4 Sherman, which was produced in greater numbers than any other tank. The Russian T-34 combined speed with endurance and was perhaps the outstanding tank of the war, playing a decisive role in the great armoured battles on the Eastern Front.

> **'Terribly noisy, oily, hot, airless and bumpy!…In action if the tank was hit slivers of hot steel began to fly…For protection we used to wear a small face mask.'**
>
> Second Lieutenant Gordon Hassell remembering conditions in a First World War tank

Above Grant tanks lined up in the Western Desert, 17 February 1942 **Below** M4 Sherman tank **Right** Detail of M4 Sherman tank in the Large Exhibits Gallery IWM E 8487

The two remaining Second World War military vehicles are a Daimler armoured car and the ubiquitous jeep, of which more than 600,000 were built.

Anti-tank weapons include the formidable *Jagdpanther* (an 8.8cm self-propelled tank destroyer) and a German 5cm anti-tank gun.

The 25-pounder was the standard British field gun of the Second World War. The 5.5-inch gun equipped British medium artillery regiments and served in all the major theatres from 1942. The *Nebelwerfer* projectile launcher was employed by Germans in considerable numbers in the later stages of the war, and the terrifying scream of its rockets was a familiar sound to Allied troops in Normandy in 1944. A 4.7-ton shell from a massive German 80cm gun is displayed. Nicknamed *Schwerer Gustav* ('Heavy Gustav'), it was the largest gun ever built but fired only 48 rounds during the war – against Sebastopol in the Soviet Union in 1942.

Naval Weapons

Above U35 in the Mediterranean, 1917 IWM Q 53010

'His devotion to duty was an example to all of us...he stayed there, standing and waiting, under heavy fire, with just his own brave heart and God's help to support him'

The captain of Jack Cornwell's ship, HMS *Chester*, writing to Jack's mother

The first British shot in the First World War was fired by the destroyer HMS *Lance* from its 4-inch gun, on display in the Large Exhibits Gallery. Another naval exhibit of note is the 5.5-inch gun from HMS *Chester* which the 16-year-old Boy First Class Jack Cornwell (left) was serving when he was mortally wounded at the Battle of Jutland in 1916. He was posthumously awarded the Victoria Cross.

By the First World War, the use of submarines and mines presented new threats to shipping. One of the weapons on display is a 10.5-cm gun from the submarine U98. Another German weapon from the First World War is a moored contact mine.

An unusual example of a Second World War submarine is the German one-man *Biber* (Beaver), which was hastily developed for operations against the Allied invasion flotilla in 1944. Another specialised underwater craft is the Italian 'human torpedo'; craft like this were employed with spectacular success against British battleships in Alexandria harbour in 1941. The *Tamzine* is the smallest surviving fishing boat to have taken part in the evacuation of British and French troops from Dunkirk in 1940.

Left Boy First Class Jack Cornwell IWM Q 20883
Below German one-man *Biber* submarine in the Large Exhibits Gallery IWM MAR 558

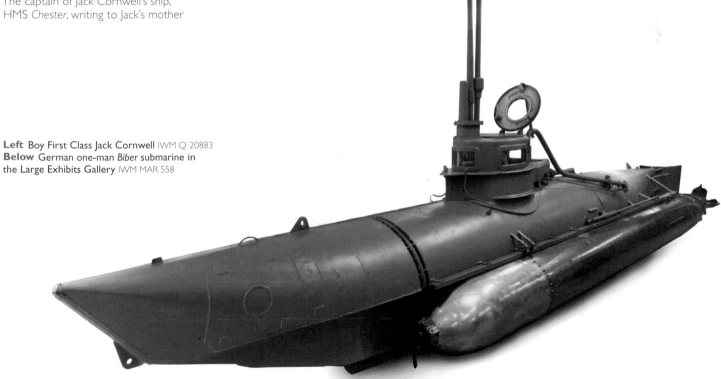

Air Weapons

The military possibilities of aircraft were not fully appreciated in 1914, but by the end of the war they had begun to exert a significant influence on the conduct of land operations. Two First World War aircraft are displayed, an early two-seat reconnaissance machine – the BE2c – and a Sopwith Camel 2F1, the naval version of the celebrated British fighter. Also on view is the observation car from a Zeppelin (probably LZ90), which was found near Colchester after an air raid in 1916.

The collection of Second World War aircraft includes a Supermarine Spitfire Mark 1A which saw action in the Battle of Britain. Another exceptional Allied fighter was the North American P-51 Mustang. With auxiliary fuel tanks it could escort bombers of the United States Eighth Air Force to Berlin and back, and it made a crucial contribution to the battle for air supremacy over Germany. German Second World War aircraft consist of a Focke Wulf 190 and a Heinkel 162. The radial-engined FW190, which the RAF first encountered in 1941, was one of the fastest and most manoeuvrable fighters of the war. The HE162 'Salamander' jet fighter was rushed into production in 1944 in a vain attempt to combat the Allied air offensive.

Above Flying goggles worn by Sergeant Thomas Mottershead (20 Squadron, Royal Flying Corps) on his final mission on the Western Front during the First World War IWM EQU 3846 **Below left** Lieutenant-Colonel JD Landers, commander of the 78th Fighter Group at Duxford, with his P-51D Mustang, 'Big Beautiful Doll', on 24 March 1945. The Museum's Mustang has been painted to represent this aircraft. IWM HU 31358 **Below right** Royal Aircraft Factory BE2c **Far Right** Sopwith Camel 2F1, Polaris A3 Missile and M3A3 Grant Tank

MUSEUM
CAFE

MUSEUM
CAFE

MUSEUM
CAFE

FOR YOUR EYES ONLY

MUSEUM
CAFE

The Holo
Exhibitio

THIRD FLOOR

The German *Vergeltungswaffen* (reprisal weapons), the V1 and V2, were launched against England in 1944. The V1, known as the 'doodlebug' or 'buzz bomb', was a pilotless aircraft with a speed of about 400 miles per hour. The V2 rocket (far left) travelled faster than sound and was impossible to intercept. A total of over 6,500 V-weapons fell on London and the South-East, killing 8,938 people.

The casing of this 'Little Boy' atomic bomb (left) is of the type dropped on Hiroshima in 1945.

The post-war Polaris was the first submarine-launched ballistic missile and was Britain's independent nuclear deterrent between 1968 and the introduction of the Trident system in 1994.

Above 'Little Boy' atomic bomb casing IWM MUN 88 **Left** German V2 Rocket in the Large Exhibits Gallery **Below left** Ruined flats in Limehouse, East London, following the explosion of the last German V2 rocket to fall on Britain, 27 March 1945 IWM HU 88803 **Below right** German V1 (Fiesler Fr 103) flying bomb IWM CL 3433

The exhibits on the First Floor above the main atrium chiefly relate to air warfare. They include a one-pounder anti-aircraft gun, which in September 1915 fired (unsuccessfully) at the first Zeppelin to raid the City of London; the cockpit sections of a Japanese Mitsubishi A6M Zero-Sen fighter and of an Avro Lancaster and a Handley Page Halifax, which together formed the backbone of the Royal Air Force's bombing offensive against Germany; a German 8.8cm high velocity anti-aircraft gun which was also used, with devastating effect, in an anti-tank role; part of the fuselage and one of the Daimler-Benz engines from the Messerschmitt 110 in which Nazi defector Rudolf Hess flew to Scotland in May 1941; and German '*Small Würzburg*' radar equipment.

Post-Second World War exhibits include a BAC Thunderbird 2, a surface-to-air guided missile designed to intercept fast, high-flying aircraft; and a 20mm twin-mounted anti-aircraft gun captured from the Argentinians during the Falklands War in 1982.

Also on this floor is the *Survival at Sea* exhibition, which tells the story of the Merchant Navy in the Second World War, including the SS *Anglo Saxon*'s jolly boat in which two merchant seamen survived for 70 days at sea and a copy of the log they kept.

The Origins and Outbreak of the First World War

Above The famous Kitchener poster, designed by Alfred Leete IWM PST 2734 **Left** The Retreat from Mons, 16th Lancers on the march, September 1914 IWM Q 56309 **Right** A recruit undergoing a medical examination IWM Q 30067

The causes of the First World War were complex and are the subject of continuing historical debate. The rise of Germany after 1871 upset the old balance of power in Europe. Tensions were heightened by conflicting national ambitions, economic competition and colonial rivalries. By 1914 an elaborate system of alliances divided Europe into two armed camps. Any incident involving one country threatened to start a chain reaction dragging them all into war. Such an incident occurred at Sarajevo in Bosnia on 28 June 1914 when the heir to the throne of Austria-Hungary, Archduke Franz Ferdinand, was assassinated. By the end of July, the armed forces of Europe were mobilising. Britain declared war on Germany on 4 August 1914, shortly after the Kaiser's armies had crossed the Belgian frontier. Britain was the only major European power without a conscript army. Field Marshal Lord Kitchener, Secretary of State for War, believed that the struggle would be long and costly. He at once set about creating volunteer 'New Armies'. By the end of 1915, nearly two and a half million men had enlisted. In 1916 Parliament passed Military Service Acts, which introduced the conscription of men between 18 and 41.

'I enlisted in a hurry because I want to go out to the front and not muck about in barracks, but it isn't plumb certain now that anybody will go'

Letter from Edward Packe to unknown recipient, 8 August 1914

The Western Front

The German bid to inflict a swift and decisive defeat on France was checked at the Battle of the Marne in September 1914. By then it had become clear that the range, accuracy and firepower of modern weapons, in particular the defensive capability of the machine gun, were such that soldiers could only survive on the battlefield by taking shelter in trenches. Attempts by each side to outflank the other failed, and by December 1914 the opposing lines of trenches extended from the English Channel to the Swiss frontier. For four years the combatants sought ways of ending the stalemate of trench warfare. On a tactical level, this resulted in successive attempts to breach the enemy trench lines by the use of massive artillery bombardments, the employment of gas and the development of the tank. Trench warfare created a world of its own – at worst, a wilderness of shattered trees, barbed wire entanglements and waterlogged craters. Soldiers on both sides often had to contend with difficulties of communication and supply, the misery of wet, cold, mud, rats and lice, and the strain of living under the ever-present threat of death or mutilation. The unprecedented number of casualties and the dreadful wounds caused by high-explosive shells stretched and challenged the medical services.

Above Trench signs IWM FEQ 366, IWM FEQ 32 **Right** The Third Battle of Ypres, 1917, Australian troops passing along a duckboard track through devastated Chateau Wood IWM EAUS 1220
Far right One of the principal features of the First World War Galleries is the *Trench Experience*. A walk-through reconstruction of a front line trench on the Somme in the autumn of 1916 is brought to life with special lighting, sound and smell effects.

War in the Air

Above Second Lieutenant Albert Ball, a photograph probably taken in 1916 IWM Q 69593 **Below left** Baron Manfred von Richthofen IWM Q 107381 **Below right** Albatros D.IIIs of von Richthofen's 'Circus' – his own red aircraft is second in line IWM Q 50328

As trench warfare settled in on the Western Front, armies became dependent upon the aeroplane as a means of discovering what the enemy was doing. Decisive combats between aircraft were rare in the early months of the war, but each side quickly saw the need to win dominance over the opposing air service. This led to the specialisation of aircraft types and hastened the development of the single-seat fighter. From 1916 the air war became a see-saw struggle for supremacy. New aircraft were introduced and tactics constantly refined and improved. By the middle of 1917, air combat had become a matter of team fighting rather than individual scouting. The best-known fighter formation was the 'Richthofen Circus', led by Baron Manfred von Richthofen (below left), an astute tactician and deadly shot, whose distinctive red Albatros became the symbol of dominance over the Western Front. Other 'aces' included the British airmen Captain Albert Ball (left), Major 'Mick' Mannock and Major James McCudden, Lieutenant-Colonel WA 'Billy' Bishop – a Canadian – and the French pilot Capitaine Georges Guynemer.

The War at Sea

Britain looked to the Royal Navy for protection against invasion and to keep the sea lanes open for essential supplies of food and raw materials. There were engagements between British warships and German commerce raiders in the Indian Ocean, the Pacific and the South Atlantic. The long-awaited clash between the British Grand Fleet and the German High Seas Fleet took place at Jutland on 31 May 1916. Although the battle was tactically indecisive, the High Seas Fleet, apart from one or two abortive sorties, remained locked in its bases for the rest of the war. The British blockade of German ports caused great hardship in Germany. The Germans retaliated by mounting a submarine campaign against Allied merchant shipping. This brought Britain close to defeat but also helped bring about America's entry into the war in April 1917 after US citizens died on torpedoed ships, notoriously the liner *Lusitania*. The adoption of the convoy system and a substantial increase in British and American shipbuilding enabled the Allies to overcome the U-boat menace.

Above Admiral Sir John Jellicoe, Commander-in-Chief of the Grand Fleet IWM Q 55499 **Below left** *The U-boats are out!*, German U-boat poster, 1917, HR Erdt IWM PST 0515 **Below right** Ships of the Grand Fleet in line ahead IWM Q 63698

The Wider War

Below left Two young Russian female soldiers stand to attention. They are part of the women's 'Battalion of Death', created by the Provisional Government in 1917 in St Petersburg. IWM Q 106252
Below right Herr von Kuhlmann signing the Treaty of Brest Litovsk which took Russia out of the First World War. Leon Trotsky, the Bolshevik Commissar for Foreign Affairs, and Count Czernin look on. IWM Q 45331

The most important theatre of the war after France was the Eastern Front, where Germany and Austria-Hungary confronted Russia and Serbia. Much was expected of the Russian 'steamroller'. But by 1917 the Russian Army had suffered enormous losses and, despite winning a notable victory against the Austrians in the summer of 1916, was exhausted and demoralised. The October Revolution ended the Russian war effort and on 3 March 1918, Russia and Germany signed a peace treaty at Brest Litovsk (below right). In addition to the Eastern Front, there were a number of subsidiary campaigns. Well over a million British, Indian, French and Dominion troops took part in campaigns against Germany's ally, Turkey – on the Gallipoli peninsula and in Egypt, Palestine and Mesopotamia. In 1915 an Allied expeditionary force, which eventually grew to 600,000 men, was landed at Salonika to oppose the Bulgarians. Following Italy's entry into the war in 1915, French and British contingents were sent to support the Italians in November 1917 after an Austro-German army had inflicted a crushing defeat on them at Caporetto. Further afield, British and German forces fought a long-running campaign in East Africa.

**'What a situation!
In front of me the
great 15" shells were
blowing the last village
in Europe to hell, and
behind the French
melinite was blasting
great holes in Asia!'**

Jack Churchill describes the Gallipoli
landings on 25 April 1915, as seen from
the battleship *Queen Elizabeth*, in a letter
to his brother Winston

Above Australian troops charge uphill with
fixed bayonets during an assault at Anzac
Cove, Gallipoli, 1915 IWM Q 13659 **Right**
African orderlies carrying a wounded man
on an improvised stretcher across a river
in German East Africa IWM Q 57601

The Home Front

The First World War had an unprecedented effect on civilian life. Shortly after the outbreak of war, the government brought in the Defence of the Realm Act, which gave it sweeping powers. News was censored, the coal mines nationalised, land and property requisitioned for military purposes, the sale of alcohol restricted and British Summer Time introduced. The changing of the clocks allowed for longer periods of daylight in the evenings, lessening the need for power for lighting and increasing the time for productivity or leisure. Food rationing was instituted in 1918. Recruiting caused labour shortages which resulted in large numbers of women doing jobs in industry, transport, agriculture and commerce previously done by men. Some 100,000 women joined the newly formed auxiliary services of the three armed forces. Zeppelin and aircraft raids caused much dislocation and put civilians in the front line for the first time. The war also made its impact on an emotional level, with almost every family being affected by the death or wounding of a relative or friend.

Above German incendiary bomb dropped by Zeppelin LZ38 on 31 May 1915 during the first airship raid on London IWM MUN 3275 **Below left** Ministry of Munitions recruitment poster, 1918 IWM PST 7703 **Below right** Men and women working in the Chilwell shell-filling factory, 1917 IWM Q 30011

Poets and Painters

The Western Front inspired some memorable poetry. The major war poets – Edmund Blunden, Siegfried Sassoon, Robert Graves, Isaac Rosenberg and Wilfred Owen – all had first-hand experience of the trenches. The direct and sometimes brutal language of their poetry has often been used to illustrate the perceived futility and tragic waste of the conflict. The war also provided powerful subject matter for artists such as John and Paul Nash, CRW Nevinson, Stanley Spencer, William Roberts and Eric Kennington. From 1916 they, and many others, were employed as official war artists to record scenes on the home and fighting fronts.

Top *We are Making a New World*, Paul Nash, 1918 IWM ART 1146 **Above** Wilfred Owen **Right** A selection of manuscripts from the extensive collection of papers of the war poet Isaac Rosenberg

What passing-bells for these who die as cattle?
– Only the monstrous anger of the guns.
Only the stuttering rifles' rapid rattle
Can patter out their hasty orisons.
No mockeries now for them; no prayers nor bells;
Nor any voice of mourning save the choirs, –
The shrill, demented choirs of wailing shells;
And bugles calling for them from sad shires.
What candles may be held to speed them all?
Not in the hands of boys, but in their eyes
Shall shine the holy glimmers of goodbyes.
The pallor of girls' brows shall be their pall;
Their flowers the tenderness of patient minds,
And each slow dusk a drawing-down of blinds.

'Anthem for Doomed Youth'
by Wilfred Owen

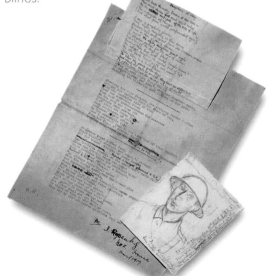

End of the War

Hostilities on the Western Front ceased at 11.00am on 11 November 1918 when an armistice between Germany and the Allies came into effect. A final settlement, determined by a peace conference, was embodied in the Treaty of Versailles, which was signed by the Germans on 28 June 1919. Germany lost territory and its armed forces were greatly reduced. It had to pay massive compensation for war damage and admit its guilt for causing the war. These terms provoked great bitterness in Germany and sowed the seeds of future discord in Europe.

Above Next of Kin Memorial Plaque. These were sent to all next of kin accompanied by a message from the King. They were colloquially known as 'dead men's pennies'. IWM EPH 2114
Below left Letters written by Emily Chitticks to her sweetheart Will Martin, who was killed on 27 March 1917. They were returned to her unopened, marked 'Killed in Action'. **Below right** Crowds waving and smiling around the Victoria Memorial outside Buckingham Palace in London on Armistice Day IWM Q 47894
Far right Silhouette of a soldier looking at a comrade's grave, Pilckem Ridge, Ypres Salient, 22 August 1917 IWM Q 2756

'I just got official notice that hostilities would cease at 11 o'clock. Everyone is about to have a fit. I fired 164 rounds at him before he quit this morning, anyway.'

Harry S Truman writing about the Armistice

The Inter-War Years

Hopes for a lasting peace after the First World War were short-lived. The next two decades witnessed a series of wars and diplomatic crises that pointed the way to a new global conflict. In Germany, Adolf Hitler established his Nazi dictatorship in 1933. Germany began to rearm, and in March 1936 Hitler reclaimed the demilitarised Rhineland and two years later marched into Austria. Shortly afterwards, at the Munich Conference, he persuaded the Western powers to force Czechoslovakia to cede the Sudetenland. In March 1939 Germany occupied the rest of Czechoslovakia. The German invasion of Poland on 1 September 1939 marked the end of the policy of Appeasement pursued by the British prime minister, Neville Chamberlain. Britain and France declared war on Germany on 3 September.

Above Model of a Nazi League of German Girls standard bearer IWM EPH 9493 **Left** A woman weeps while giving the Nazi salute at the start of the German occupation of the Sudetenland IWM NYP 22525 **Below left** Nazi election poster. The slogan reads 'Only Hitler'. IWM PST 3301 **Below right** Adolf Hitler addressing the Nazi party rally at Nuremberg, 1936 IWM (MOI) FLM 1531

The Second World War

Above Doris and Alan Suter step down into the Anderson air raid shelter in the garden of their home. Alan is carrying his gas mask box with him. IWM D 778 **Below left** British troops wading out to a rescue ship off Dunkirk, 1940 IWM HU 41240 **Below right** German Heinkel He IIIs IWM MH 6547

Following the defeat of Poland, which was overwhelmed in a campaign lasting only four weeks, Britain and France were faced with the prospect of a long and costly war with Germany. Britain braced itself for an all-out German attack, and civil defence plans were put into effect. Although there was some action at sea, there was little activity on land or in the air. The war developed a sense of unreality which earned it the title of the 'Phoney War'.

In the spring of 1940, Germany launched Blitzkrieg (lightning war) attacks in Scandinavia and Western Europe. German forces invaded Norway and Denmark in April and the Low Countries and France on 10 May – the day on which Winston Churchill became prime minister. The main German attack was directed not against the heavily fortified Maginot Line but through the lightly defended Ardennes (lightly defended because it was seen as impassable). German tanks and assault troops with close air support broke through the French line and drove northwards towards the sea, splitting the Allied armies in two. The British Expeditionary Force and the French First Army were cornered at Dunkirk, but 338,000 men managed to escape, thanks to a hasty but effective evacuation operation mounted across the English Channel. The German advance against the bulk of the French forces continued until an armistice was agreed on 22 June.

The Battle of Britain

Above Adolf Hitler and his senior commanders during a planning conference at the Berghof, July 1940. Hitler explains a point with the aid of maps to (left to right) General Franz Halder and Field Marshals Walther von Brauchitsch and Wilhelm Keitel. General Alfred Jodl stands, with folded arms, at the head of the table. IWM HU 75533 **Below left** The Battle of Britain, 1940. Pattern of condensation trails left by British and German aircraft after a dog fight. IWM H 4219 **Below right** Detail from a German invasion map for Operation 'Sealion', 1940

After the collapse of France, Britain, her Commonwealth and Empire stood alone. In July 1940 Hitler directed that plans be drawn up for an invasion of the British mainland, codenamed Operation 'Sealion'. But before the invasion could be mounted, the Germans had to compensate for their weakness at sea by defeating the RAF and winning command of the skies over the South of England. The Luftwaffe began its main offensive on 13 August 1940, attacking airfields, radar stations, ports and aircraft factories. Fighter Command was down to its last reserves when, on 7 September, the assault was unexpectedly switched to London. The Luftwaffe's efforts intensified but so did its losses. On 17 September, defeated in the air and out-gunned at sea, Hitler postponed 'Sealion' indefinitely.

'Never in the field of human conflict was so much owed by so many to so few'

Winston Churchill's tribute to the Royal Air Force, House of Commons, 20 August 1940. The Battle of Britain peaked a month later.

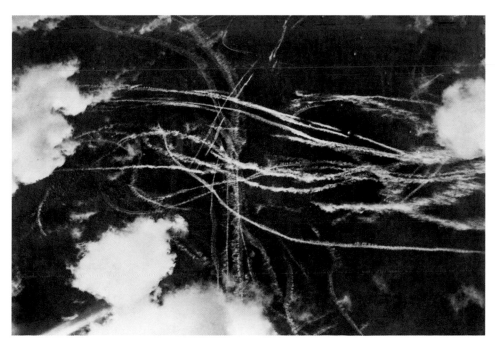

The Home Front

Above The weekly ration for two
people, UK, 1943 IWM D 14667 **Below
left** *Women of Britain – Come into the
Factories*, Philip Zec, c.1941 IWM PST 3645
Below right The *Blitz Experience* in the
Museum **Far right** The Elephant and
Castle underground station in South
London, 11 November 1940
IWM D 1568

**Unable to launch an invasion, Germany tried instead to bomb
Britain into submission**. The Blitz, the period of most sustained
bombing, lasted from September 1940 until the late spring of 1941. London
was attacked on 57 consecutive nights, and 15 other British cities, notably
Coventry, suffered extensive damage. Over 41,000 British civilians were
killed and 137,000 injured. Britain came under heavy attack again in 1944
from Germany's secret weapons, the V1 and the V2. The country endured
not only air raids but also severe shortages of food and raw materials. Life
in Britain was hard and drab. Every kind of resource was mobilised for the
war effort. The conscription of men and women into civil as well as military
occupations was introduced: by the middle of 1944, over 460,000 women
were in the services and six and a half million were engaged in civilian war
work. Britain became home to thousands of refugees as well as foreign
servicemen. Later, hundreds of thousands of Americans arrived once
preparations began for an Allied invasion of Europe.

WOMEN OF BRITAIN
COME INTO THE FACTORIES
ASK AT ANY EMPLOYMENT EXCHANGE FOR ADVICE AND FULL DETAILS

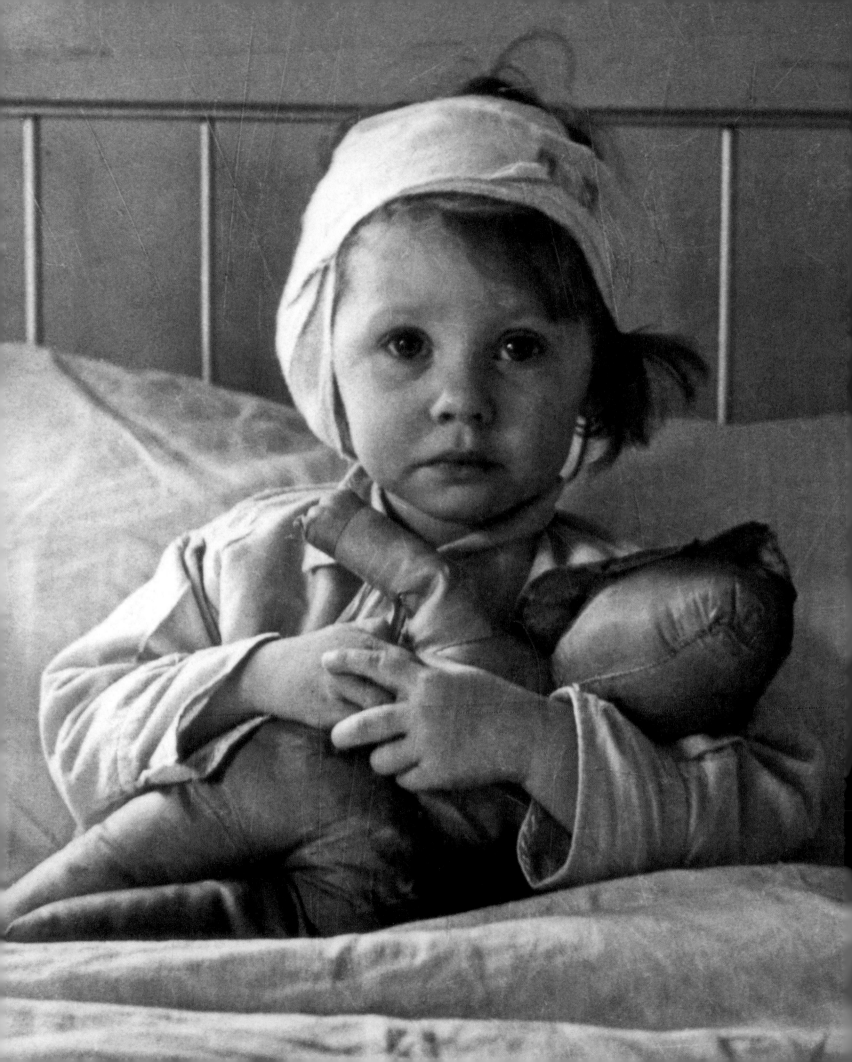

The Children's War and the 1940s House

This exhibition looks at the Second World War through the eyes of British children. It provides a unique and moving insight into the impact of the war on those who lived through it – from the evacuees who were forced to adjust to separation from family and friends, to the children who stayed in towns and cities to endure the horror of the Blitz.

Over the course of the Second World War, some 130,000 children suffered the loss of a parent on active service; 1,000,000 were evacuated from their homes (with a further 16,000 sent overseas); and 7,736 children died as a direct result of enemy action.

The stories of these children are told through their letters, books, toys and games, and a number of other mementoes which illustrate the devastating impact of war at all levels.

Visitors have the opportunity to explore a life-size 1940s house and can also see a prefabricated home, introduced after the war as a quick replacement for bombed houses.

Above Letter in *The Children's War* sent from a girl to her father **Left** Three-year-old Eileen Dunne in the Hospital for Sick Children,1940, photographed by Cecil Beaton IWM MH 26395
Below The *1940s House*

The War at Sea Against Germany and Italy

For Britain, dependent upon imports, command of the sea was vital. The German surface fleet, which eventually included the battleships *Bismarck* and *Tirpitz* as well as other powerful modern warships, represented a constant menace to Allied merchant shipping; in the event it did relatively little damage. The flow of raw materials, food, munitions and men from North America was the key to Britain's survival. As in the First World War, German submarines posed the biggest threat to the supply routes. The U-boats inflicted losses averaging 96 ships a month in 1942, but by the middle of 1943 the Battle of the Atlantic had swung in favour of the Allies. Better anti-submarine weapons and detection devices, trained convoy support groups, small aircraft carriers designed for convoy escort work and long-range aircraft all helped to defeat the U-boats. Shipping in the Mediterranean and convoys carrying Allied supplies to Russia were also at risk.

Top *The British Navy*, Frank Mason, c.1941 IWM PST 0067 **Above** The carriers *Indomitable* and *Eagle* during Operation 'Pedestal', (a convoy to the beseiged island of Malta in 1942) IWM A 15961 **Right** Model of a German Type VII U-boat IWM MOD 662

Mediterranean and Middle East

Above British sailors and British and American soldiers on the beach near Algiers, November 1942 IWM A 12719
Below right General Montgomery in his Grant tank. This tank is displayed in the Large Exhibits Gallery.
IWM E 18980 (KT)

As Germany completed the domination of Western Europe, fighting began in the Mediterranean theatre. German forces swept through Greece in the spring of 1941, and an airborne invasion of Crete forced British troops to evacuate the island. Earlier, an Italian attack on Egypt had been successfully repulsed, but the German Afrika Korps, sent to reinforce the Italians early in 1941, posed a new threat in the Western Desert under the aggressive leadership of General Rommel. After 18 months of fighting, in June 1942 Rommel captured the important port of Tobruk. Two months later, Lieutenant-General Montgomery took command of the British Eighth Army and ended its series of defeats by winning a decisive victory at the Battle of El Alamein in November. Operation 'Torch', the landing of Allied troops under the command of General Eisenhower, led in May 1943 to the surrender of the Axis forces in North Africa. The capture of Sicily in August 1943 and the subsequent invasion of Italy gave the Allies their first foothold on the European mainland since 1940. German forces seized control of the remainder of Italy when the Italians agreed to an armistice with the Allies. From this point the Allied advance through Italy was slow and costly, but by the spring of 1945 the Allies had reached the north Italian plains. The German forces in Italy surrendered unconditionally on 2 May.

'I've got to go to meet God – and explain all those men I killed at Alamein'

Field Marshal Viscount Montgomery, near the end of his life in 1976

Eastern Front

Strategic, economic and ideological motives lay behind Hitler's decision to order the invasion of Russia. The German offensive, Operation 'Barbarossa', began on 22 June 1941, taking the Soviet forces by surprise. Employing well-tried Blitzkrieg tactics, the three-million-strong force struck deep into the Soviet heartland, capturing whole Russian armies before coming to a halt on the outskirts of Leningrad and Moscow. In December 1941 the Soviet Union surprised the Germans by mounting a counter-offensive, easing the pressure on Moscow. Hitler turned his attention to the south and attacked in the Caucasus in the spring of 1942. His armies were comprehensively defeated at Stalingrad early in 1943 and in the Battle of Kursk in the summer, which cost the Wehrmacht half a million men. The Germans, fighting doggedly, were steadily driven from Soviet territory at the cost of 27 million Russian lives.

Above German straw 'snow' boots used on the Eastern Front IWM UNI 12917 **Left** Russian infantry advancing during the Soviet winter offensive of 1942 IWM RUS 2109 **Below left** Russian patriotic poster using imagery from the Czarist period as well as communist symbolism IWM PST 0183 **Below right** German Panzer Mark III and assault troops, a photograph probably taken in the Ukraine in 1941 IWM COL 158

Europe Under the Nazis

Above Improvised tools made by POWs at Colditz to build a glider as a means of escape **Right** Colditz Castle © Dr Reinhold Eggers IWM HU 63855 **Below** An example of a Red Cross parcel sent to British prisoners of war in Germany during the Second World War **Far right** Members of the Dutch underground movement IWM BU 2887

In the wake of German victory came Nazi exploitation of the conquered territories. Occupied Europe's agricultural and industrial output was channelled to meet Germany's needs, regardless of the deprivation this caused. The Nazis imposed repressive racial and political policies. Although the severity of German rule varied greatly from country to country, no community remained untouched. The first attempts at resistance in Occupied Europe were largely isolated and ill-coordinated acts of personal opposition. But with the passage of time, men, women and children joined together to confront their oppressors. An alternative to Nazi propaganda was provided by the illegal press. Escape lines and intelligence networks helped the Allied war effort. Where circumstances permitted, resisters carried out a guerilla war against the German and collaborationist forces. However, effective armed resistance was largely dependent on support from one of the Allies' own clandestine organisations.

The Bomber Offensive

Above Air Chief Marshal Sir Arthur Harris IWM CH 13020

The strategic air offensive was intended to bring Germany to its knees by attacking its economic strength and will to resist. The ineffectiveness of operations up to the end of 1941 exposed the weakness of the RAF. Aircraft, bombs and navigational equipment were inadequate, and losses in daylight raids caused Bomber Command to switch to night attacks. From February 1942 Air Chief Marshal Harris (left) adopted the 'area' bombing of German cities in an attempt to disrupt industrial production and morale. On 31 May 1942, the first 'thousand bomber' raid was launched against Cologne. In August 1942 the American Eighth Air Force joined the offensive and began precision daylight bombing against key targets. In 1943 and 1944 the RAF attacked the Ruhr, Hamburg and Berlin. Enemy fighters took a heavy toll and German war production actually increased until July 1944. The arrival of long-range escort fighters transformed the bomber offensive in the last phase of the war. A Bomber Command attack in support of Allied land operations culminated in the destruction of the historic city of Dresden in February 1945, causing thousands of civilian deaths. The bomber offensive was extremely costly, with Bomber Command losing 55,573 aircrew and 1,570 ground staff.

Above American B-17 Flying Fortresses IWM HU 4052 **Right** Dresden, photographed a few years after the war © Gotz Bergander IWM A 3321 **Far right** *An Air Gunner in Action Turret: Night* (detail), Keith Henderson OBE, 1940 IWM ART LD 633

North-West Europe

Above British Commando troops going ashore on D-Day, 6 June 1944 IWM B 5103
Below left Instrument of Surrender dated 4 May 1945, signed by the German delegation on Luneburg Heath in the presence of Field Marshal Montgomery IWM U 52168 **Below right** The signing of the Instrument of Surrender at 21st Army Group Headquarters, Lüneburg Heath, 4 May 1945 IWM BU 5207

In 1944 the Eastern Front turned increasingly in Russia's favour, and in June the Allied invasion of Normandy opened the campaign for the liberation of Western Europe. On 6 June 1944 ('D-Day'), Operation 'Overlord' began, under the American Supreme Commander, General Eisenhower. The assault forces, under the command of General Montgomery, came ashore from some 4,000 landing craft escorted by 600 warships, with air support from more than 10,000 Allied aircraft. Over 156,000 British, Canadian and American troops were landed on the first day, making this the largest amphibious operation in history. After a month of heavy fighting, Caen fell to the British and Canadians. At the end of July, American forces broke through the German defences and advanced rapidly south and east. Paris was liberated on 25 August, Brussels on 3 September. Montgomery's bold plan to open a 'back door' into Germany through Holland ended in failure on 26 September when the British 1st Airborne Division was almost annihilated in an attempt to seize a vital river bridge at Arnhem. A daring German counter-attack, of questionable value, in the Ardennes in December was repulsed, and in March 1945 Allied troops crossed the Rhine. As agreed at the Yalta Conference in February 1945, the Western Allies halted on the Elbe, allowing the Russians to take Berlin.

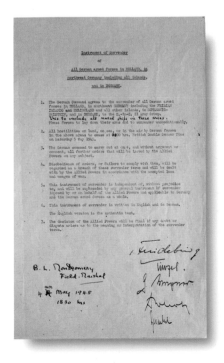

Below Two British sailors and their girlfriends wading in the fountains in Trafalgar Square on VE Day
IWM EA 65799

In the last months of the war, Hitler's mental and physical health deteriorated rapidly, and on 30 April he committed suicide in his underground bunker. On 4 May German forces in North-West Europe surrendered to the Commander-in-Chief of the 21st Army Group, Field Marshal Montgomery. The instrument of Germany's unconditional surrender was signed at Eisenhower's headquarters in Rheims on 7 May. Victory in Europe (VE) Day was celebrated the following day.

War in the Far East

Above British mortar team in action, Imphal-Kohima, July 1944 IWM INDA 4723 **Below** *Prisoner Ill with Dysentery, Changi Gaol* Ronald Searle, 1944 IWM ART 15747 134

By 1941 Japanese ambitions in Asia and the Pacific had led to a serious deterioration in relations with the United States. On 7 December 1941, without a declaration of war, Japanese carrier-borne aircraft attacked the US Pacific Fleet at its base at Pearl Harbor in the Hawaiian Islands. Congress declared war on Japan the next day. The Allies were ill-prepared to defend their possessions in the Far East, and by the summer of 1942 the Japanese had overrun the Philippines, Malaya, Burma and the Dutch East Indies (modern Indonesia). Japan's early successes resulted in the capture of hundreds of thousands of Allied military personnel and civilians who had to endure malnutrition, disease, forced labour and appalling living conditions. Over a quarter of them died.

American General MacArthur's forces fought their way through New Guinea to the Philippines; in another series of operations the Solomon Islands were recaptured after savage resistance by the Japanese. In the central Pacific, Admiral Nimitz carried out a series of amphibious operations which brought the Americans within bombing range of Tokyo. In the Battle of Imphal-Kohima in 1944, the British Fourteenth Army under General Slim won a decisive victory which removed the Japanese threat to India. By the spring of 1945, the Americans were preparing to invade Japan. President Truman decided to use the newly developed atomic bomb to end the war. Two bombs were dropped – on Hiroshima on 6 August 1945 and on Nagasaki three days later. On 14 August the Japanese surrendered unconditionally.

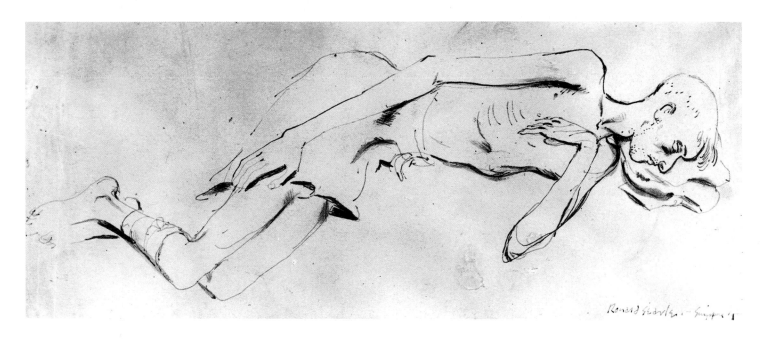

Left The atomic explosion at Nagasaki, 9 August 1945 IWM MH 2629 Above Items recovered from Hiroshima and Nagasaki including a bottle melted and crushed by the atomic explosion at Hiroshima IWM EPH 4630, IWM EPH 4631, IWM FEQ 317

Conflicts Since 1945

Left A section of the Berlin Wall owned by the Museum **Right** The Korean War; a North Korean villager from Yongaong-Ni passes a radio operator of 1st Battalion, The Middlesex Regiment IWM BF 182

The end of the Second World War did not bring an end to conflict. There has been fighting somewhere in the world almost every day since 1945.

Post-war divisions between Eastern and Western Europe led to a prolonged Cold War. The development of the atomic bomb precipitated a nuclear arms race, with both sides possessing the means to destroy the world. The collapse of communism in Europe, marked by the pulling down of the Berlin Wall in 1989 and the break-up of the Soviet Union, ended the Cold War and diminished the threat of nuclear war in the West.

Elsewhere in the world, the ending of colonial rule and attempts to prevent the spread of communism led to fighting in many countries. During the Cold War period, the US and the Soviet Union tried to exert their influence in other parts of the world and sometimes prolonged or complicated existing conflicts.

In Asia China, North Korea and North Vietnam came under communist control, and communists in Malaya made a bid for power. Some of the largest and longest post-war conflicts followed. America led the fight against communism, but British and Commonwealth forces fought in Korea and Malaya, and Australian and New Zealand forces fought alongside the Americans and South Vietnamese in the Vietnam War.

Left A column of Royal Marines from 45 Commando march towards Port Stanley, 13–14 June 1982 IWM FKD 2028
Right British 1st Armoured Division, First Gulf War, 1991 (Mike Moore Collection) IWM GLF 633

In Africa the granting of independence to former colonies was often accompanied or followed by fighting and civil war. Famine and disease among the many refugees was a major cause of loss of life.

Disagreements over territory and access to oil fields have led to conflict in the Middle East. Britain's political influence in this region declined after the Suez Crisis of 1956. Iraq's seizure of Kuwait in 1990 was countered by the formation of a multinational coalition force. During the First Gulf War, Britain made a major contribution, with the largest deployment of its forces on active service since the Second World War. The coalition protected Saudi Arabia, also under threat of an Iraqi invasion, and in 1991 ejected the Iraqis from Kuwait.

Britain's armed forces have undergone major changes since 1945. National Service ended in 1963, after a reduction in Britain's colonial commitments and the development of an independent nuclear deterrent. Unexpected crises such as the Argentine invasion of the Falklands in 1982 required a rapid military response from Britain. Longer-term deployments of British forces have included commitments in Northern Ireland, and, increasingly, a peacekeeping role, often under the auspice of the United Nations or NATO. Although the gallery displays end with the First Gulf War, the Museum continues to collect material relating to current deployments, notably in Afghanistan and Iraq.

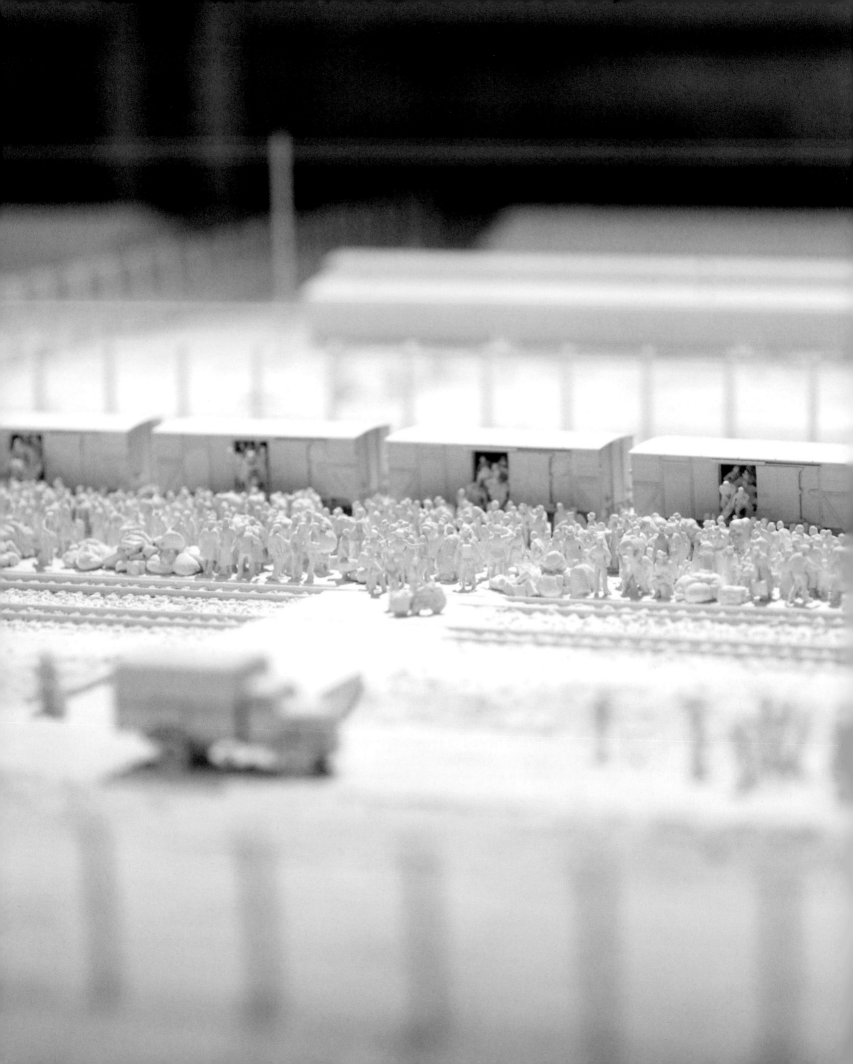

The Holocaust Exhibition

Above Jews from Bedzin, Poland. Only five people in this photograph survived the Holocaust. Courtesy Mrs Helen Stone
Left Model of Auschwitz (detail) in *The Holocaust Exhibition*

The Holocaust Exhibition traces the Nazi persecution and murder of Europe's Jews from 1933 to 1945. It also covers other groups targeted by the Nazis, such as Gypsies (Roma and Sinti), Poles, Soviet prisoners of war after 1941, the disabled, Jehovah's Witnesses and homosexuals. Arranged over two floors, the exhibition uses original artefacts, documents and film, much of which has never been seen in this country. Specially recorded testimony from 16 Holocaust survivors provides a poignant personal insight.

The exhibition is situated on two floors:

Upper Floor The November 1918 Armistice brought peace, but Europe was left scarred and in economic depression. In Germany there was resentment of what was seen as a punishing peace treaty, and many blamed the Jews for the country's defeat.

1920–1933 saw the steady rise of the new National Socialist German Workers Party – the Nazi Party – led by Adolf Hitler. In 1933 Hitler became Chancellor of Germany, and a reign of terror began, with political opponents sent to concentration camps. The first major anti-Jewish measure, a boycott of Jewish businesses, took place on 1 April 1933.

Central to Nazi ideology was antisemitism, a centuries-old prejudice which was prevalent throughout Europe. The Nazis saw themselves as a 'Master Race' and wanted to cleanse Germany – and Europe – of 'alien' influences, including Jews and Gypsies. From 1933 anyone alleged to be disabled or mentally 'unfit' was sterilised – a measure intended to prevent the contamination of the 'Aryan' race. The Nazis used propaganda to spread hatred of Jews and passed antisemitic legislation which stripped Jews of citizenship and progressively barred them from professions. Only during the Berlin 1936 Olympic Games was this public hostility to the Jews relaxed for foreign visitors.

Above *One People, One Reich, One Führer,* a 1938 Nazi poster IWM PST 8398

This exhibition is not recommended for children under 14. Parents or carers wishing to take younger children into the exhibition may do so at their own discretion. Children must be closely supervised at all times.

'We were actually made into sub-humans'

Holocaust survivor Freddie Knoller

Top Jewish-owned shop on the Potsdamer Strasse in Berlin, damaged during *Kristallnacht* Courtesy BPK Berlin, Germany **Above** Identity card of a Jewish woman stamped with a 'J' under a 1938 Nazi regulation

From March 1936, Hitler set about reclaiming the lands lost after the First World War and expanding Germany's borders. German troops entered the Rhineland, Austria, the Sudetenland, then the rest of Czechoslovakia and Memel in Lithuania. Jews in these territories began to suffer and many sought refuge abroad.

On 9 November 1938, Nazi stormtroopers rampaged through Germany's streets, attacking Jewish businesses and killing 91 Jews – an event known as *Kristallnacht* (the Night of Broken Glass). With violence now an ever-present threat, many more Jews sought desperately to emigrate, but most countries would admit only limited numbers in a time of economic hardship. Some 50,000 came to Britain, 10,000 under the *Kindertransport* scheme which brought unaccompanied children to this country. War broke out on 1 September 1939 when Hitler invaded Poland. In October Hitler ordered the killing of thousands of mentally ill and disabled people. They were murdered by gas or lethal injection in the first Nazi mass murder programme.

Lower Floor Germany swiftly conquered much of Poland, with Soviet troops securing Eastern Poland. In the reign of terror that followed, thousands of Poles were murdered, and Jews were especially singled out. They were stripped of property, made to do forced labour and concentrated in ghettos. Details of Nazi crimes reached Britain, usually through couriers working for the Polish government-in-exile based in London. Then, in June 1941, Germany invaded the Soviet Union. SS murder squads – *Einsatzgruppen* – shot entire Jewish communities, often assisted by local volunteers. In two days, nearly 40,000 Jews were shot at Babi Yar, on the outskirts of Kiev. In the ghettos of occupied Poland, Jews either worked for rations or smuggled food in a desperate attempt to stay alive. Conditions worsened, however, and 500,000 Jews eventually died from disease or hunger. In March 1942 the Nazis began to move people out of the ghettos for 'Resettlement in the East': a euphemism for deportation to death camps.

In an attempt to find a more efficient killing method, the Nazis started to murder Jews with gas, first in vans, and then in chambers at four death camps – Chelmno, Belzec, Sobibor and Treblinka. Rumours of the camps reached the ghettos. In Warsaw, the Jews revolted against the Nazis. Starving and with few weapons, they held out for a month before being killed or captured. Prisoners at Sobibor and Treblinka also staged revolts.

Above Yellow star of a Dutch Jew

From September 1941, Jews in Nazi-occupied countries were forced to wear a yellow star. This preceded large-scale deportation to camps in packed railcars, often without food or water. Some Jews were hidden by non-Jewish friends or family; others were betrayed. Timetables were co-ordinated to transport Jews speedily to their deaths.

The last, and largest, death camp to go into operation was Auschwitz II-Birkenau. One million Jews, thousands of Gypsies and other victims were murdered in its gas chambers. As the trains arrived, Jewish victims were selected by an SS doctor. About one in five was sent for slave labour, the rest gassed immediately. Auschwitz was one of an immense system of camps in Nazi-occupied territory in which Jews not killed on arrival joined other prisoner groups deemed enemies of the Reich. Life expectancy was short.

The news of the extermination of Jews led to calls for action. The general response of the Allied governments was that the way to save lives was to win the war.

As the Nazis retreated before the Soviet advance, they tried to hide evidence of their crimes, destroying camps and digging up and burning the remains of thousands of their victims. Prisoners were force-marched to camps inside the Reich. Thousands died on these 'death marches'.

Majdanek, captured by the Soviet Army in July 1944, was the first concentration camp to be liberated. The Allies did not reach most camps until April 1945, among them Bergen-Belsen, where British troops found the largest single grouping of Jewish survivors. The reports sent from these camps horrified the world. Although trials of war criminals were held, many perpetrators escaped justice.

The Holocaust Exhibition concludes with the words of the survivors whose stories have been heard at intervals throughout the display. They tell us what effect their experiences have had on their lives and of their hope that mankind will learn from this most terrible event of modern times.

Top Arrival of Hungarian Jews in Auschwitz II-Birkenau *Courtesy Yad Vashem Archives, Israel* **Above** Shoes taken from prisoners at Majdanek concentration camp *Courtesy Panstwowe Muzeum na Majdanku, Lublin, Poland*

It is easy to mistake spy fiction for reality...

Secret War

The Secret War exhibition reveals the clandestine world of espionage, covert operations and the work of Britain's special forces.

The exhibition shows how Britain's secret government agencies, MI5 and MI6, have developed since their establishment before the First World War, and how specialist communications technology has been used to gather intelligence and break top-secret codes. The work of the Special Operations Executive is covered through exhibits and film footage which provide an insight into the training SOE agents received to enable them to operate in enemy-held territory in the Second World War. Among the exhibits are bottles of invisible ink used by German spies in the First World War, an original German Enigma cipher machine (left), codebooks, SOE sabotage devices and a secret radio used by MI6 agents during the Cold War. Files on individual agents and operations can be accessed through interactive videos.

Above Enigma enciphering machine IWM COM 228 **Left** *Secret War* **Below left** Rubber soles designed by SOE and worn under agent's boots to disguise footprints during beach landings **Below right** Long Range Desert Group Chevrolet 30-cwt truck

The exhibition also looks at the history of highly trained elite special forces such as the Special Air Service and the Long Range Desert Group. It includes firearms and equipment used in the Second World War and in more recent conflicts such as the Falklands and the Gulf. There are two dramatic audio-visual presentations: *The Benina Raid*, a daring SAS and Long Range Desert Group attack on a German airfield in North Africa in 1942, and a reconstruction of Operation 'Nimrod', the SAS operation to release hostages held in the Iranian Embassy in London in 1980.

Victoria and George Cross Gallery

The Victoria Cross and George Cross Gallery houses the Museum's collection of these supreme awards for military and civil gallantry. The centrepiece of the display is the 13-pounder 'Néry' gun and the three VCs awarded to its crew after the Battle of Mons. The stories of Boy First Class Jack Cornwell, Lieutenant JD Smyth (later Brigadier the Rt Hon Sir John Smyth), Corporal Charles Garforth, Group Captain Leonard Cheshire and other First and Second World War VCs are told. Among the George Crosses are those awarded to the SOE agent and resistance hero Wing Commander FFE Yeo-Thomas (the 'White Rabbit'), and to Lieutenant Robert Davies, who saved St Paul's by defusing a bomb which fell close to the cathedral during the Blitz. Related exhibits include a telescope used by Lieutenant Augustus Agar VC and a beret belonging to Colonel 'H' Jones VC.

Above Victoria Cross (left), George Cross (right) **Below** The Victoria Cross and George Cross Gallery **Far Right** Lance Corporal William Hewitt, who was awarded the Victoria Cross for his actions during the Third Battle of Ypres in September 1917

Art Galleries

Above *Continuous Profile (Head of Mussolini)*, Renato Bertelli, 1933 © Giorgio Bertelli IWM ART LD 5975 **Left** *Gassed* (detail), John Singer Sargent, 1919 IWM ART 1460 **Below left** *Ready To Start. Self Portrait,* Sir William Orpen RA, 1917 IWM ART 2380 **Below right** *Skull in a Landscape,* Edward Burra, c.1946 © Edward Burra Estate, c/o LeFevre Fine Art, London IWM ART 15554

The two suites of galleries on the second floor are used for long-term exhibitions of First and Second World War works of art from the Museum's collection. The displays are changed at regular intervals. Works of art are also lent to exhibitions at other galleries. If coming to the Museum to see a particular painting, it is advisable to telephone the Department of Art beforehand to check that the work is available. Details of temporary exhibitions are available in the Reception area and online.

The art collection is rich in modern British painting by most of the leading war artists of the twentieth century, including Sir William Orpen, Sir John Lavery, Sir George Clausen, Augustus John, Sir Stanley Spencer, Paul Nash and John Nash, Percy Wyndham Lewis, William Roberts, CRW Nevinson and Eric Kennington. The art of the Second World War (which also includes work by Paul Nash and Kennington) was dominated by Henry Moore, Graham Sutherland, John Piper, Anthony Gross, Thomas Hennell, Edward Ardizzone and Edward Bawden, all of whom are represented in the collection.

In addition, there are significant holdings of work by Carel Weight, Mervyn Peake, Evelyn Dunbar and Richard Eurich. Recent acquisitions have included works by Edward Burra, Cecil Collins, John Tunnard and Keith Vaughan.

One of the most famous paintings in the Museum's collection, *Gassed* by John Singer Sargent (left), is shown in the Sargent Room.

Collections Highlights

IMPERIAL WAR MUSEUM
Weekdays 10-5 50 Sundays 2-5 50 Lambeth Road London SE1 6HZ

Underground Lambeth North or Elephant and Castle

Above Imperial War Museum Poster,
Tom Eckersley, 1981 *Courtesy of University
of the Arts London (reference TE/1/12)*
IWM PST 9202

Above Toy bear belonging to Paul
Sondhoff, a Jewish boy hidden from
the Nazis for four years in a cupboard
by his piano teacher in Vienna
Courtesy the Foster family

**The Imperial War Museum provides extensive access to its
'behind the scenes' Collections**. No other museum in the world has a
similar breadth of material covering all aspects of twentieth-century conflict
and beyond. You can arrange to visit, write to the appropriate department
or use the website (**www.iwm.org.uk**) for further information.

The Department of Art holds one of the leading collections of British
twentieth-century art. It is rich in fine and graphic art and is especially strong
in works commissioned for official purposes during the two world wars.
The latter are complemented by the papers of the War Artists' Archive. The
sculpture collection includes works by Charles Sargeant Jagger and Jacob
Epstein. Altogether there are 14,000 works of fine art. The collection of
some 30,000 international war posters is unparalleled in Britain.

The Department of Documents is a major repository for the private
papers, amounting to 11,500 collections, of those involved in warfare. It holds
the diaries, letters and papers of individuals of all ranks and status, military
and civilian. These include manuscript material of the work of war poets
and writers such as Isaac Rosenberg and Siegfried Sassoon. Second World
War foreign records, a significant source of information on the military and
economic history of Germany, Italy and Japan, and the records of the major
war crimes trials held by the Allies in Nuremberg and Tokyo are also available.

The Department of Exhibits and Firearms holds an astonishing
variety of objects, including artillery, badges, communications equipment,
currency, edged weapons, ephemera, flags, firearms, medals and models,
toys, transport and uniforms. The displays at all our branches offer the
best insight into the variety of objects held by the Museum.

The Film and Video Archive is one of the oldest documentary film
archives in the world; the collection ranges almost from the birth of cinema
to the present and offers detailed coverage of the military, political and
social history of the twentieth century. The Film and Video Archive holds
120 million feet of film and 6,500 hours of video tape. Much of the material
on the two world wars is 'official' in origin, derived from British government
and military initiatives to generate material for publicity and record purposes.
There are also contemporary collections, such as the former library of
NATO headquarters in Brussels and extensive footage received from UNTV
Zagreb covering the conflict in former Yugoslavia. The collection includes a
number of privately shot 'home movies' of life in wartime.

Above Wounded men of the 1st Battalion, Lancashire Fusiliers, being tended in a trench in the 29th Division's area near Beaumont Hamel on the morning of the initial assault of the Battle of the Somme, 1916 IWM Q 739

Above First World War song sheet: *I ain't got weary yet! Je m'un fais pas encore*, Pub New York, Leo. Feist Inc. 1918 'Patriotic war edition' Acc No: K94/1012

The Photograph Archive is one of the largest specialised archives in the UK and one of the most accessible. It has over six million photographs. Coverage of the two world wars reflects the heyday of black and white photography in the first half of the twentieth century; colour photography begins to take over in more recent conflicts. The archive is international in scope, although British and Commonwealth material predominates. American involvement in both world wars is well covered. The work of professional and private photographers complements the large official collections.

The Department of Printed Books is a national reference library on twentieth-century conflict involving Britain and Commonwealth countries. It has some 100,000 books, 25,000 pamphlets, 15,000 volumes of periodicals, and 15,000 maps and technical drawings. Its resources include rare books, official publications, unit histories, journals, maps and much fascinating printed ephemera such as aerial propaganda leaflets, prisoner of war material, pamphlets and miscellanea. The department is the best starting point for visitors interested in tracing family history. The Museum does not hold individual service records but can help in a general way.

The Sound Archive is a pioneer in the field of oral history. It now holds some 35,000 hours of interviews and recordings and offers the researcher a huge array of experience to draw on. Coverage has been built up by topic and selection influenced by the 'race against time' to record reminiscences before it is too late. There are special collections on particular themes such as the Spanish Civil War and the Holocaust.

For further information ask for the free booklet:
The Collections: An Access Guide

The UK National Inventory of War Memorials' archive holds information about 56,000 British war memorials. The project database can be viewed by appointment in the Museum's Reading Room, or online at www.ukniwm.org.uk.

General Information

Opening Hours
Open daily from 10.00am – 6.00pm
Closed 24, 25, 26 December

Access for Study:
Weekdays 10.00am – 5.00pm

Saturday Study Service:
Documents and Printed Books only

Admission Free

There may be a charge for some special exhibitions

General Enquiries and Information
Enquiries 020 7416 5000
Fax 020 7416 5374
Email mail@iwm.org.uk
www.iwm.org.uk
Imperial War Museum
Lambeth Road, London SE1 6HZ

Education Service
The Museum's Education Centre provides excellent facilities for a wide range of activities including talks, study sessions, drama, art, films and sixth-form conferences on the two world wars, the Holocaust and conflict since 1945. Please visit the website for further details, or call 020 7416 5313.

Group Bookings
Groups are classified as ten or more people. For all group bookings and enquiries, please contact the Bookings Officer on 020 7416 5439 (Mon–Fri, 10.00am – 5.00pm) or email groups@iwm.org.uk.

Mailing List
For free, up-to-date information about exhibitions and events, visit the Imperial War Museum's website www.iwm.org.uk, telephone 020 7416 5439 or email list@iwm.org.uk.

Facilities for Disabled Visitors
All areas of the Museum are accessible to wheelchairs except the first floor of the *1940s House* in *The Children's War* exhibition. Please telephone 020 7416 5000 for further information or download an Access Guide from the website.

Friends of the Imperial War Museum
Membership benefits include special events, a magazine and free admission to all Imperial War Museum branches and charging exhibitions. For further information, telephone 020 7416 5255 (office hours).

Hospitality and Conferences
For facilities and hire charges, telephone 020 7416 5393 (office hours).

Comments and Suggestions
Suggestions for improving our service are welcomed. Please write to the Visitor Services Officer or complete a Comments Form, available from the Information Desk.

Shopping
Visitors to the Museum Shop can enjoy browsing our extensive range including books, DVDs and CDs, prints and postcards, educational resources, and a large selection of gifts and souvenirs for all ages. Our Online Shop can be found at www.iwmshop.org.uk.

The Imperial War Museum is a charity and all profit from sales of these products supports the work of the Museum.

Support Us
The Museum welcomes donations, including legacies, to help it continue its work. As a supporter of the Imperial War Museum, you would be helping us to inspire learning and encourage debate through our unparalleled programme of educational activities and the care, conservation and exhibition of our extensive Collections. To find out how you or your company can support our invaluable work, please contact the Development Department. Telephone 020 7091 3042 or email iwmdevelopment@iwm.org.uk, or to make a donation online visit www.iwm.org.uk.